FINANCIAL INDEPENDENCE, RETIRE EARLY (FIRE)

STRATEGIES AND PERSONAL FINANCE TIPS FOR ACHIEVING EARLY RETIREMENT

DR. DENISE E. GREAVES

Copyrighted © 2024 by Denise Greaves

All rights reserved. No part of this publication may be reproduced, distributed, or transmitted in any form or by any means, including photocopying, recording, or other electronic or mechanical methods, without the prior written permission of the author, except in the case of brief quotations embodied in critical reviews and certain other noncommercial uses permitted by copyright law. For permission requests, write to the author at the address below.

Email: drdenisewrites@gmail.com

First Edition

Printed in the United States of America

ISBN: 979-8-9912006-1-5

Limit of Liability/Disclaimer of Warranty

The author has endeavored to ensure the accuracy and completeness of the content contained in this book; however, no warranties, either express or implied, are made regarding the performance or results that may be achieved from following the guidance provided herein. The information is provided on an "as is" basis, and the author disclaims all responsibility for any loss or damage caused by the use of this book.

No legal or financial advice is being provided, and readers are advised to consult with a professional for specific advice tailored to their situation. The author shall not be liable for any loss of profit or any other commercial damages, including but not limited to special, incidental, consequential, or other damages.

The author does not endorse and is not responsible for the accuracy or reliability of any opinion, advice, or statement made through the book by parties other than the author. Nor is the author responsible for any offensive, defamatory, or illegal conduct of other users of the book or third parties. Readers' reliance on any information provided by this book is solely at their own risk.

Synopsis:

Dive into the heart of financial independence with Pathways to FIRE, a comprehensive guide designed to equip you with the knowledge, strategies, and insights needed to retire early and live on your own terms. Written by Denise Greaves, a seasoned expert in personal finance, this book unravels the complexities of saving, investing, and budgeting in a clear and actionable way.

What You Will Learn:

- Strategies to Maximize Your Savings: Discover proven methods to enhance your income and radically increase your savings rate.

- Investment Insights for Long-Term Growth: Learn how to build and maintain a diversified investment portfolio that stands the test of time.

- Practical Budgeting Techniques: Gain control over your finances by mastering budgeting techniques that pave the way for financial freedom.

- Psychological Aspects of Early Retirement: Navigate the mental and emotional challenges associated with stepping away from traditional work life.

For Whom:

Whether you're just starting out in your financial journey or are halfway there, Pathways to FIRE is essential reading for anyone dreaming of a life less ordinary—free from the constraints of traditional employment and full of possibilities.

"Financial freedom is not a dream for the future; it is a decision for today. Start your journey to FIRE and live on your own terms."

TABLE OF CONTENTS

Preface 9
Acknowledgments 11
Chapter Summaries 12
Chapter 1: Introduction to FIRE 15
    Understanding the FIRE Movement 15
    The Importance of Financial Independence 16
    Benefits of Early Retirement 16
Chapter 2: Setting the Foundation 18
    Assessing Your Financial Situation 18
    Net Worth Calculation Table 19
    How to Use This Table: 19
    Example: 20
    Defining Your FIRE Goals 21
    Creating a Financial Roadmap 21
Chapter 3: Budgeting for FIRE 25
    Tracking Your Expenses 25
    Sample Spreadsheet Template for Expense Tracking .. 27
    Instructions for Use 27
    Customizing Your Template 28
    Cutting Unnecessary Costs: Strategies 28

Chapter 4: Maximizing Income 31
    Increasing Your Salary 31
    Side Hustles and Passive Income Streams 32
    Entrepreneurship for Financial Independence 33
Chapter 5: Investing for Growth 35
    Understanding Different Investment Options 35
    Stocks, Bonds, and Mutual Funds 36
    Real Estate Investment 36
    Diversifying Your Portfolio 37
Chapter 6: Tax Optimization 39
    Understanding Tax-Advantaged Accounts 39
    Tax-Efficient Investment Strategies 40
    Leveraging Deductions and Credits 40
Chapter 7: Frugality and Minimalism 42
    Embracing a Frugal Lifestyle 42
    Minimalist Living for Financial Independence 43
    Distinguishing Needs from Wants 43
Chapter 8: Debt Management 46
    Strategies for Paying Off Debt 46
    Good Debt vs. Bad Debt 47
    Staying Debt-Free 48
Chapter 9: Healthcare Planning 50
    Understanding Healthcare Options 50
    Managing Healthcare Costs 51

Long-Term Care Planning 51
Chapter 10: Retirement Planning 53
    Calculating Your Retirement Number 53
    Safe Withdrawal Rates 54
    Planning for Inflation 54
Chapter 11: Psychological Aspects of FIRE 56
    Dealing with Social Pressures 56
    Maintaining Motivation 57
    Mental Health and Financial Stress 57
Chapter 12: Creating a FIRE-Friendly Lifestyle 59
    Building a Supportive Community 59
    Staying Active and Engaged 60
    Adjusting Lifestyle Costs 60
Chapter 13: Tools and Resources for Achieving FIRE 62
    Financial Independence Calculators 62
    Sample FIRE Tracker Template 63
    Instructions for Use 63
    Visualization 65
    Recommended Books and Blogs 65
    Useful Apps and Software 66
    Forums and Online Communities 66
Chapter 14: Conclusion 68
    Staying the Course 68
    Continual Learning and Adaptation 69

Living a Fulfilled and Independent Life 69
Wrapping Up 69
Special Thanks 71

PREFACE

Welcome to a journey that goes beyond the traditional narratives about personal finance and retirement. This book is designed for anyone who has ever dreamed of stepping away from the conventional path to discover a life of freedom, purpose, and financial independence. Whether you're in the early stages of your career, nearing what many consider the standard retirement age, or somewhere in between, the principles of Financial Independence, Retire Early (FIRE) offer a compelling alternative to the prescribed life script.

The concept of FIRE is simple yet radical: save and invest aggressively so that you can retire decades earlier than the traditional retirement age. However, the implementation of this concept is anything but simple. It requires discipline, strategic planning, and, most importantly, a mindset shift about what it means to truly live and work on your terms.

In this book, I aim to demystify the process of achieving financial independence. You will find a blend of foundational theories, actionable strategies, and personal insights drawn not only from my experiences but also from those who have successfully navigated this path. We'll explore the nuances of budgeting, saving, investing, and managing expenses in ways that align with achieving early retirement. Additionally, this book addresses the psychological and lifestyle adjustments necessary for embracing and sustaining a life of financial freedom.

The decision to write this book came from a combination of personal passion and a desire to fill a gap in the existing literature about FIRE. While there are many resources about personal finance, few tackle the concept of retiring early in a comprehensive manner. This book is written for the pragmatist and dreamer alike, offering a clear, detailed roadmap and inspiring you to take action.

As we embark on this journey together, I invite you to challenge your assumptions, ask questions, and consider how the principles discussed might be adapted to your personal circumstances. My hope is that by the end of this book, you will not only have a deeper understanding of how to achieve financial independence but also be inspired to start taking steps toward creating the life you truly desire.

Thank you for picking up this book and taking the first step toward a different kind of future. Let's begin.

ACKNOWLEDGMENTS

Writing this book has been an incredibly rewarding journey, and reaching its conclusion would not have been possible without the support and encouragement from a circle of exceptional individuals.

First, I extend my deepest gratitude to my family and friends for their unwavering support and patience throughout the process of writing this book. Their constant encouragement and the personal sacrifices they've made have allowed me the time and space necessary to bring this project to fruition.

I am profoundly thankful to the many members of the FIRE community who have generously shared their insights and personal stories. These contributions have been invaluable, not only in enriching the content but also in demonstrating the real-world applicability of the principles discussed in this book.

Special thanks go to my editor, whose keen insights and suggestions have greatly enhanced the clarity and flow of this work. Your guidance has been indispensable in shaping the final manuscript into something we can all be proud of.

Lastly, I am grateful to the financial experts and mentors who have inspired and guided me over the years. Your wisdom and teachings have been the foundation upon which this book was built.

Thank you for joining me on this journey.

CHAPTER SUMMARIES

1. Introduction to FIRE

This chapter introduces the concept of Financial Independence, Retire Early (FIRE), explaining its origins and the core principles. It discusses the psychological and practical benefits of achieving financial independence and the freedom it provides.

2. Setting the Foundation

Learn how to evaluate your current financial situation and set realistic FIRE goals. This chapter guides you in creating a comprehensive financial roadmap to reach your early retirement objectives.

3. Budgeting for FIRE

Discover the importance of budgeting in the FIRE journey. This chapter provides strategies for tracking expenses, reducing unnecessary costs, and implementing an effective savings plan.

4. Maximizing Income

Explore ways to increase your income through salary negotiations, side hustles, passive income streams, and entrepreneurship. Learn how diversifying income sources can accelerate your path to financial independence.

5. Investing for Growth

Understand various investment options, including stocks, bonds, mutual funds, and real estate. This chapter emphasizes the importance of a diversified portfolio and offers investment strategies for long-term growth.

6. Tax Optimization

Learn about tax-advantaged accounts, tax-efficient investment strategies, and how to leverage deductions and credits to maximize your savings and reduce your tax burden.

7. Frugality and Minimalism

Adopt a frugal and minimalist lifestyle to fast-track your FIRE journey. This chapter helps you distinguish between needs and wants, promoting a simpler, more cost-effective way of living.

8. Debt Management

Effective strategies for paying off debt and maintaining a debt-free lifestyle are covered in this chapter. Understand the difference between good and bad debt and learn how to manage both.

9. Healthcare Planning

Plan for healthcare costs and insurance options in retirement. This chapter covers health insurance, managing healthcare expenses, and planning for long-term care needs.

10. Retirement Planning

Calculate your retirement number and understand safe withdrawal rates. This chapter helps you plan for inflation and ensures your retirement funds last throughout your lifetime.

11. Psychological Aspects of FIRE

Address the psychological challenges of pursuing FIRE, including dealing with social pressures, maintaining motivation, and managing financial stress. Learn strategies to stay focused and positive.

12. Creating a FIRE-Friendly Lifestyle

Build a supportive community and stay active and engaged during your FIRE journey. This chapter encourages you to pursue hobbies and passions that align with your financial independence goals.

13. Tools and Resources

Discover a range of tools and resources to assist you in your FIRE journey, including financial independence calculators, recommended books and blogs, and useful apps and software.

14. Conclusion

The final chapter emphasizes the importance of staying the course, continually learning, and adapting to new challenges. It encourages you to live a fulfilled and independent life post-retirement.

This book aims to be a comprehensive guide to achieving financial independence and early retirement, providing practical advice, and a roadmap for anyone interested in joining the FIRE movement.

CHAPTER 1

INTRODUCTION TO FIRE

Welcome to the exciting first step on your journey toward Financial Independence, Retire Early (FIRE). This movement isn't just about escaping the 9-to-5 grind; it's about redefining what it means to live and work on your terms. Whether you dream of exploring new hobbies, traveling the world, or simply spending more time with loved ones, FIRE opens the door to possibilities that traditional retirement paths might delay for decades.

In this opening chapter, we'll dive into what the FIRE movement is, explore its roots, and understand the core principles that fuel its passionate community. By seeing how others have successfully navigated this path, you'll gain both inspiration and practical insights to start your own journey with confidence. Let's light the match together and set your financial future ablaze with potential and promise!

Understanding the FIRE Movement

The Financial Independence, Retire Early (FIRE) movement is a lifestyle philosophy centered on achieving financial independence (FI) and the option to retire early (RE). The core principle is simple: save and invest aggressively so that you can live off the passive income generated by your investments sooner than traditional retirement ages allow.

The origins of FIRE trace back to the 1990s, with roots in the frugality and simple living movements. It gained significant traction in the 2010s through blogs and books that detailed personal journeys toward financial independence. Today, it is a global phenomenon embraced by countless individuals seeking control over their time and financial destiny.

The Importance of Financial Independence

Financial independence is defined as the state where one has sufficient personal wealth to live without the need to work actively for basic necessities. For many, achieving financial independence is about more than just escaping the 9-to-5 grind; it's about security, flexibility, and the freedom to pursue one's interests and passions without financial constraints.

One of the key attractions of financial independence is its empowerment. Being financially independent means being insulated from many of the economic shocks that can disrupt lives, such as layoffs or medical emergencies. It also provides a substantial psychological benefit, reducing stress related to financial insecurity.

Benefits of Early Retirement

Early retirement is often misunderstood as simply stopping work. However, in the context of FIRE, it refers to the freedom to choose how to spend your time, including changing careers, starting a business, or focusing on volunteer work, without the pressure of earning a specific income.

The benefits of retiring early include:

- **Health and Well-being**: Leaving the workforce can reduce stress and physical demands, leading to improved mental and physical health.

- **Pursuit of Passions**: With financial independence, individuals can pursue interests and passions that may not have been feasible while working full-time.

- **Increased Family Time**: Early retirement can provide more time to spend with family, raise children, or care for aging parents.

- **Opportunity for New Ventures**: Many who achieve FIRE use their freedom to start new ventures or dive deep into hobbies that could turn into income-generating activities.

The Path to FIRE

Achieving FIRE requires meticulous planning and a disciplined approach to saving and investing. While the idea may seem daunting, the path to FIRE is made accessible by breaking it down into achievable steps:

1. **Expense Management**: Understanding and controlling where your money goes is critical.

2. **Income Maximization**: Increasing your income through career growth, side hustles, or passive income.

3. **Smart Investing**: Building a portfolio that grows and protects your wealth over time.

4. **Lifestyle Choices**: Adopting a lifestyle that balances enjoyment today with financial goals for tomorrow.

Conclusion

The journey to FIRE is not just about financial planning; it's a transformational process that encourages individuals to rethink their relationship with money, work, and life priorities. By embracing the principles of the FIRE movement, you gain the tools and knowledge to construct a life that is not only financially secure but also rich in personal fulfillment.

CHAPTER 2

SETTING THE FOUNDATION

Embarking on the path to Financial Independence, Retire Early (FIRE) is like preparing for a grand adventure—it all begins with a solid foundation. This chapter is your guide to laying the groundwork for your financial journey, a critical step that will help shape the success of all your endeavors toward achieving early retirement.

Here, we'll assess your current financial landscape, define clear and achievable FIRE goals, and develop a personalized financial roadmap. Think of this process as constructing a blueprint for your dream home. Each financial decision and strategy you implement is akin to placing a brick, with the ultimate goal of building a sturdy, secure structure that will stand the test of time.

Together, we'll navigate through the essentials of financial planning, from understanding your cash flow and net worth to setting strategic, long-term objectives. Ready to roll up your sleeves and start building? Let's pave the way to a future where you are not just financially secure, but also free to live life on your terms.

Assessing Your Financial Situation

The journey towards financial independence begins with a thorough assessment of your current financial situation. This is crucial for understanding your starting point and setting realistic goals. Begin by creating a detailed inventory of your assets, liabilities, income, and expenses.

- **Assets**: Include everything of value you own, such as savings accounts, retirement funds, real estate, and personal property.
- **Liabilities**: List all debts and financial obligations, including mortgages, car loans, student loans, and credit card balances.
- **Income**: Document all sources of income, including your salary, rental income, dividends, and any side business revenue.
- **Expenses**: Track every expense over a period, ideally for at least one month, to understand where your money goes. Categorize expenses into necessities (housing, utilities, food, health care) and discretionary spending (entertainment, dining out, hobbies).

Using this information, calculate your net worth by subtracting your total liabilities from your total assets. This number provides a snapshot of your financial health and will serve as a baseline to track your progress towards FIRE.

Here's a simple table format you can use to organize and calculate your net worth:

Net Worth Calculation Table

Category	Description	Amount
Assets		
Cash	Checking accounts, savings accounts	$X
Investments	Stocks, bonds, mutual funds, retirement accounts	$X
Real Estate	Primary residence, other properties	$X
Personal Property	Vehicles, jewelry, art	$X
Other Assets	Business interests, etc.	$X
Total Assets		**$Total A**
Liabilities		
Mortgage	Home loan	$X
Student Loans	Education loans	$X
Auto Loans	Car loans	$X
Credit Cards	Total credit card debt	$X
Other Liabilities	Personal loans, etc.	$X
Total Liabilities		**$Total L**
Net Worth	Total Assets - Total Liabilities	**$Net Worth**

How to Use This Table:

1. **Fill in the Amounts**: Start by listing the current balances of all your assets and liabilities. Be as accurate as possible and use the most recent statements and assessments.

2. **Calculate Total Assets and Liabilities**: Sum up all the amounts under the Assets column to get your Total Assets. Do the same for the Liabilities column to determine your Total Liabilities.

3. **Subtract Liabilities from Assets**: To find your net worth, subtract the Total Liabilities from the Total Assets. The formula is:

Net Worth=Total Assets−Total Liabilities

Example:

Suppose your financial breakdown is as follows:

- **Cash**: $5,000
- **Investments**: $50,000
- **Real Estate**: $200,000
- **Personal Property**: $25,000
- **Other Assets**: $20,000
- **Mortgage**: $150,000
- **Student Loans**: $25,000
- **Auto Loans**: $10,000
- **Credit Cards**: $5,000
- **Other Liabilities**: $5,000

The calculation would look like this:

Category	Amount
Total Assets	$300,000
Total Liabilities	$195,000
Net Worth	$105,000

Use this table to provide a clear snapshot of your financial status and to help you track your progress towards achieving financial independence as you work on increasing your assets and decreasing your liabilities.

Defining Your FIRE Goals

With a clear understanding of your financial situation, you can begin to define your FIRE goals. These goals should be specific, measurable, attainable, relevant, and time-bound (SMART). Consider what financial independence means to you and when you would like to achieve it. Common goals include:

- **Savings Rate**: Determine the percentage of your income that you can save and invest. Many in the FIRE community aim for a savings rate of 50% or higher.

- **Investment Targets**: Set targets for investment account balances that will generate enough passive income to cover your living expenses.

- **Debt-Free Date**: If you have significant debt, set a realistic date for when you aim to be debt-free, excluding a mortgage if that's part of your long-term strategy.

Creating a Financial Roadmap

Creating a financial roadmap is like drawing a detailed map for a long journey. It involves not just knowing the destination but understanding the route, potential obstacles, and milestones along the way. Here's how to develop a comprehensive financial roadmap that is deeply integrated with your FIRE goals and your current financial situation:

1. Budget Optimization

Your budget is the cornerstone of your financial roadmap. Begin by refining the budget you developed when assessing your financial situation. Link this directly to your savings and investment goals by allocating specific percentages of your income to different categories:

- **Essentials**: Aim to keep essential expenses (housing, food, healthcare) below 50% of your income.

- **Savings and Investments**: Depending on your FIRE timeline and lifestyle choices, target a savings rate that accelerates your journey; commonly 50% or more of your net income.

- **Discretionary Spending**: Limit or adjust discretionary spending to ensure it aligns with your values and doesn't detract from your FIRE goals.

2. Debt Management Plan

Your debt reduction strategy should connect directly to your budget. Use the surplus from your optimized budget to tackle debts, focusing on:

- **High-Interest Debt**: Prioritize debts with the highest interest rates to reduce total interest paid over time (debt avalanche method). This typically includes credit card debts and personal loans.

- **Small Balances**: Alternatively, for psychological wins, start by paying off smaller debts to feel progress and maintain motivation (debt snowball method).

- **Link to Investments**: As debts are paid off, redirect the funds that were used for payments into investments, maintaining your momentum towards financial growth.

3. Investment Strategy Development

Developing an investment strategy is essential for building the wealth needed to achieve FIRE. Your strategy should reflect your risk tolerance, investment horizon, and specific FIRE goals:

- **Retirement Accounts**: Maximize contributions to tax-advantaged accounts like 401(k)s and IRAs to reduce your taxable income and grow your investments tax-free.

- **Index Funds and ETFs**: Allocate a significant portion of your investments to low-cost index funds or ETFs. These provide broad market exposure, reducing risk and requiring less active management.

- **Real Estate and Other Investments**: Consider diversifying into real estate or other income-generating assets if they align with your skills and interests. Real estate, for example, can provide both rental income and capital appreciation.

4. Setting Milestones

Milestones are crucial for keeping your journey on track and maintaining motivation. They should be measurable, achievable, and linked to your broader financial goals:

- **Short-term Milestones**: These might include saving your first $10,000, paying off a specific debt, or reaching a six-month emergency fund.

- **Long-term Milestones**: Set targets like achieving a $1 million investment portfolio, owning a fully paid-off property, or reaching a specific net worth.

5. Regular Review and Adjustment

The financial landscape and your personal circumstances will change over time, necessitating regular reviews of your roadmap:

- **Quarterly Reviews**: Every three months, review your budget, check your progress against milestones, and assess investment performance. Adjust your allocations or strategies as needed.

- **Annual Reviews**: Conduct a comprehensive annual review that includes reassessing your financial goals, risk tolerance, and life situation (e.g., changes in family, job, health).

Each component of your financial roadmap is interconnected. Effective budgeting increases your capacity to repay debts and invest. Successful investments increase your net worth, bringing you closer to FIRE. Regular reviews ensure that each part of your plan is working harmoniously towards your ultimate goal of financial independence and early retirement.

This approach of creating a financial roadmap ensures that your financial actions are not just isolated decisions but are part of a cohesive strategy designed to lead you to financial independence and enable you to retire early, should you choose to do so.

Conclusion

Setting a strong foundation is critical for your success in the FIRE journey. By thoroughly assessing your financial situation, defining clear and meaningful goals, and creating a detailed financial roadmap, you equip yourself with the tools necessary to navigate towards financial independence and early retirement. This chapter serves as the groundwork upon which the subsequent strategies and tips in the book will build, ensuring you have a solid base from which to grow your financial future.

CHAPTER 3

BUDGETING FOR FIRE

Welcome to Chapter 3, where we turn our focus to one of the most powerful tools in your financial toolkit—budgeting. As you pursue Financial Independence, Retire Early (FIRE), mastering your budget is not just about monitoring where your money goes; it's about strategically directing it to serve your greatest goals and dreams.

In this chapter, we'll break down the process of creating a budget that not only fits your current lifestyle but also accelerates your progress towards FIRE. Think of your budget as your personal financial GPS. Just as a GPS guides you on the road, your budget guides your financial decisions, ensuring you stay on the path to early retirement.

From tracking your daily expenses to identifying opportunities to boost your savings, we'll explore practical strategies and tips that make budgeting both effective and sustainable. Ready to take control of your finances and make your money work harder for you? Let's dive in and build a budget that powers your journey to financial independence!

Tracking Your Expenses

Tracking your expenses meticulously is crucial for identifying where your money goes and where you can potentially cut costs. Detailed tracking allows you to align your spending with your financial goals, especially important in the journey to Financial Independence, Retire Early (FIRE). Here are detailed methods to effectively track your expenses:

1. Digital Tools and Apps

Using financial apps is a convenient way to automatically track your expenses. Here are some popular ones:

- **Mint**: Connects to your bank accounts, categorizes your transactions automatically, and provides visual insights into your spending patterns.

- **You Need A Budget (YNAB)**: Emphasizes giving every dollar a job, ideal for proactive budgeters who want to align their spending with specific financial goals.

- **Personal Capital**: Offers investment tracking alongside regular expense tracking, which is great if you're also managing a portfolio.

These tools often provide features like budget setting, reminders, and reports that analyze your spending over time, making it easier to identify trends and adjust your habits.

2. Spreadsheet Tracking

For those who prefer a hands-on approach or wish to customize their expense tracking, spreadsheets are a powerful tool. Here's how to set up an effective spreadsheet for expense tracking:

- **Categories**: Create columns for different expense categories such as housing, groceries, transportation, utilities, entertainment, and dining out.

- **Dates and Details**: Include a date for each expense entry and a brief description to remind you of each transaction.

- **Monthly Summaries**: Use formulas to sum up expenses in each category per month. This helps in comparing monthly spending and spotting trends or anomalies.

- **Annual Overview**: Implement a summary sheet to assess your spending habits annually, which is helpful for long-term financial planning.

Sample Spreadsheet Template for Expense Tracking

Here's how you might structure the spreadsheet:

Sheet 1: Monthly Expenses

Date	Description	Category	Amount ($)	Payment Method
2024-07-01	Electricity Bill	Utilities	120.00	Auto-debit
2024-07-03	Groceries	Food	85.00	Credit Card
2024-07-05	Monthly Train Pass	Transportation	60.00	Cash
2024-07-08	Dinner Out	Dining	45.00	Credit Card
...	...	...	...	...

Sheet 2: Monthly Summary

Category	Budgeted Amount	Actual Spent	Difference
Utilities	150.00	120.00	30.00
Food	400.00	385.00	15.00
Transportation	100.00	60.00	40.00
Dining	150.00	200.00	-50.00
...	...	...	...

Sheet 3: Annual Overview

Month	Total Income	Total Expenses	Savings
January	3,000.00	2,500.00	500.00
February	3,000.00	2,600.00	400.00
March	3,200.00	2,400.00	800.00
...	...	...	...
Total	36,000.00	30,000.00	6,000.00

Instructions for Use

1. **Monthly Expenses Sheet**: Enter each expense as it occurs. This real-time tracking helps in maintaining accurate records of your spending.

2. **Monthly Summary Sheet**: At the end of each month, total your expenses by category and compare them against your budgeted amounts. This will help you identify areas where you are overspending or underspending.

3. **Annual Overview Sheet**: Summarize your monthly income, expenses, and savings to get an overview of your financial health across the year. This helps in assessing your overall progress toward your financial goals.

Customizing Your Template

- **Add or Remove Categories**: Tailor the expense categories to reflect your personal spending habits for more accurate tracking.

- **Adjust Payment Methods**: Include additional columns if you use various payment methods like digital wallets, bank transfers, etc.

- **Set Budget Alerts**: If using an advanced spreadsheet tool like Google Sheets or Excel, you can set up conditional formatting to alert you when spending exceeds budget in a particular category.

This template will serve as a robust tool in managing your finances, helping you to stay aware of your spending and make informed decisions that align with your FIRE goals.

Templates like Google Sheets or Microsoft Excel have built-in budgeting and expense tracking templates that you can customize according to your needs.

3. Manual Receipt Collection

If you're less tech-inclined or prefer tangible records, keeping receipts and logging them manually into a notebook or ledger can be effective. This method forces you to confront each expense physically, which can make you more aware of spending habits.

Cutting Unnecessary Costs: Strategies

Once you have a clear picture of your spending, you can start identifying and eliminating unnecessary costs. Here are strategies to help reduce your expenses:

1. Evaluate Recurring Expenses

Many people incur on-going costs for services they rarely use. Evaluate each subscription and recurring service:

- **Subscriptions**: Analyze all subscriptions (magazines, streaming services, apps). Cancel anything that isn't essential or regularly used.

- **Memberships**: Gym memberships, clubs, or other memberships should be evaluated. If you haven't visited the gym in months, it might be time to cancel.

2. Reduce Utility Bills

Utilities can be a significant monthly expense, but they offer opportunities for savings:

- **Energy Efficiency**: Invest in energy-efficient appliances, LED lighting, and smart thermostats to reduce energy bills.

- **Water Savings**: Install low-flow showerheads and fix any leaks to cut down on water usage.

- **Evaluate Plans**: Periodically review your phone, internet, and cable plans. Switch to more economical plans or negotiate with your providers for better rates.

3. Mindful Spending

Develop habits that encourage more mindful spending:

- **Wait Period**: Implement a 24-hour or 48-hour wait period before making non-essential purchases to avoid impulse buying.

- **Needs vs. Wants**: Regularly assess whether an expense is a need (essential) or a want (non-essential). Prioritize needs and scrutinize wants.

- **Cash Diet**: Use cash for discretionary spending categories like eating out and entertainment. Once the cash set aside for the month is gone, no more spending in that category.

Conclusion

Getting a handle on your expenses and cutting back on unnecessary costs isn't just about numbers and budgets—it's about reclaiming your financial freedom and taking charge of your future. Each dollar you save and redirect towards your investments brings you one step closer to achieving the dream of Financial Independence, Retire Early (FIRE).

As you become more aware of your spending habits and learn to prioritize your financial goals, you'll find that budgeting becomes less of a chore and more of a rewarding challenge. It's about making mindful choices that align with your values and long-term visions. Remember, every small change you make has a compound effect on your financial health.

Embrace this process with enthusiasm and curiosity. Celebrate your successes, no matter how small, and learn from the setbacks without discouragement. Share your journey with others who might be on a similar path; you'll find that community support is invaluable. Your efforts today are laying the groundwork for a life where work is optional, and your time is truly yours.

Keep pushing forward, stay motivated, and let your budget be a living document that grows and adapts with you. Here's to making empowered financial decisions and living a life full of both purpose and freedom!

CHAPTER 4

MAXIMIZING INCOME

Welcome to Chapter 4, where we focus on boosting the fuel for your FIRE journey—your income. While managing expenses is crucial, increasing what you earn can dramatically accelerate your path to Financial Independence, Retire Early (FIRE). In this chapter, we'll explore various avenues to enhance your earnings, from negotiating a higher salary to uncovering opportunities for passive income.

Whether you're looking to climb the career ladder, start a side hustle, or delve into entrepreneurship, each strategy we discuss is designed to not only increase your financial inflow but also enrich your professional and personal life. The goal here is to empower you with the tools and confidence needed to seize opportunities and maximize your earning potential.

Ready to boost your income and speed up your journey to financial freedom? Let's get started by exploring practical, actionable strategies that can make a significant impact on your finances.

Increasing Your Salary

Achieving Financial Independence, Retire Early (FIRE) often requires more than just cutting costs; increasing your income is equally crucial. One of the most direct ways to do this is by focusing on your primary income source—your salary.

- **Negotiate Your Salary**: Regularly review your salary in the context of your industry and your contributions to your company.

Prepare for negotiations by documenting your achievements, understanding the market rate for your role, and developing negotiation skills.

- **Seek Promotions**: Aim for higher positions within your company that come with increased salaries. Understand the qualifications needed for these roles and work on acquiring them, whether through internal training, additional education, or taking on more responsibilities.

- **Change Jobs**: Sometimes the fastest salary increase can come from changing companies. Look for opportunities in companies that offer higher pay for your skills or are known for their career development opportunities.

Side Hustles and Passive Income Streams

In addition to optimizing your salary, developing side hustles or passive income streams can significantly boost your total income.

- **Freelancing**: Use your current skills to freelance in your spare time. Platforms like Upwork, Freelancer, or Fiverr can connect you with clients needing services ranging from graphic design to programming to writing.

- **Starting a Side Business**: Consider a small business that you can manage in your spare time. This could be something as simple as lawn care, tutoring, or an online store.

- **Real Estate**: Investing in rental properties can provide a steady source of passive income. Start with a single property and expand as you gain more experience and capital.

- **Investing in Dividend Stocks**: Build a portfolio of stocks that pay dividends. This is a way to earn passive income from your investments, and if reinvested, can significantly compound over time.

Entrepreneurship for Financial Independence

For those who aspire to fully control their income potential, entrepreneurship can be a powerful path.

- **Start a Business**: Identify a market need and launch a business that addresses it. This could be related to a personal passion or a professional gap you've observed.

- **Scale Your Business**: Focus on creating systems and processes that allow your business to operate without your constant involvement. This scalability can eventually lead to significant passive income.

- **Exit Strategy**: Consider your long-term strategy for the business, which might include selling it. A successful exit can provide a substantial financial boost towards achieving FIRE.

Investing in Yourself

An often-overlooked aspect of maximizing income is investing in yourself. This includes education, professional development, and maintaining a healthy work-life balance.

- **Continuing Education**: Attend workshops, take courses, or pursue additional certifications that can increase your marketability and professional value.

- **Networking**: Build and maintain professional relationships that could lead to opportunities for advancements or leads for your side projects.

- **Health and Wellbeing**: Maintain a healthy lifestyle, including regular exercise, a balanced diet, and sufficient rest. A healthy body and mind can lead to improved productivity and motivation.

Conclusion

As you navigate through the strategies outlined in this chapter, remember that maximizing your income isn't just about the numbers; it's about empowering yourself to make choices that enrich your life and bring you closer to your dreams of financial independence and early retirement. Every extra dollar you earn and save is a step towards more freedom and choices in the future.

I encourage you to approach this journey with creativity and enthusiasm. Whether it's confidently asking for the raise you deserve, diving into a new side hustle with excitement, or embracing the challenge of entrepreneurship, each effort is a building block towards your larger vision. Celebrate each victory, no matter how small, and learn from each setback without losing heart.

Connect with others who share your goals, share your experiences, and seek advice when needed. The path to FIRE is not just a solo endeavor but a community journey enriched by the stories and support of like-minded individuals. Your proactive steps today are not just for financial gain but for crafting a life of meaningful work, passion, and ultimate freedom.

Stay curious, stay driven, and let each new stream of income fuel your journey to a life where work is an option, not a necessity. Here's to creating a future that resonates with your deepest aspirations!

CHAPTER 5

INVESTING FOR GROWTH

Welcome to Chapter 5, the heart of your journey toward Financial Independence, Retire Early (FIRE). Here, we delve into the exciting world of investments—a crucial component in building and sustaining wealth. Whether you're new to investing or looking to refine your portfolio, this chapter is designed to demystify the process and show you how to make your money work for you.

Investing can seem daunting with its jargon and the perceived risk, but it's also one of the most effective ways to grow your assets and secure your financial future. We'll explore various investment avenues, from stocks and bonds to real estate and mutual funds, providing you with the knowledge to make informed decisions that align with your FIRE goals.

As we navigate through the principles of effective investing, remember that this is not just about growing wealth—it's about creating the freedom to live your life on your terms. Let's set the stage for a prosperous future where you can enjoy the fruits of your investments and the lifestyle you've envisioned. Ready to take the next step in your financial adventure? Let's dive in!

Understanding Different Investment Options

To achieve Financial Independence, Retire Early (FIRE), it's crucial to understand and utilize various investment vehicles. Each type of investment offers different benefits and risks, and a well-rounded portfolio can help you grow your wealth steadily and securely.

- **Stocks**: Purchasing shares of a company gives you a stake in its earnings and assets. Stocks are known for their potential for high returns, but they also come with volatility and market risk.

- **Bonds**: When you buy bonds, you are lending money to a corporation or government in exchange for periodic interest payments plus the return of the bond's face value when it matures. Bonds are generally safer than stocks but offer lower returns.

- **Mutual Funds**: These are investment programs funded by shareholders that trade in diversified holdings and are managed by professionals. Mutual Funds are less risky than individual stocks because they are diversified.

- **Exchange-Traded Funds (ETFs)**: Similar to mutual funds, ETFs are collections of stocks or bonds, but they trade on an exchange like a stock. They offer the benefits of diversification and lower fees.

Stocks, Bonds, and Mutual Funds

Investing in these traditional assets can be a solid foundation for your investment portfolio:

- **Risk and Return Balance**: By balancing stocks and bonds, you can manage the overall risk and potential return of your portfolio. Typically, stocks are higher risk with higher potential returns, while bonds provide steady, less volatile income.

- **Diversification**: Mutual funds and ETFs provide instant diversification, which helps reduce risk by spreading investments across various assets.

Real Estate Investment

Real estate can be another vital component of your investment strategy:

- **Rental Properties**: Owning rental properties provides regular income and potential appreciation in value. The key is to find properties in high-demand areas where rental income can cover mortgages and other expenses.

- **Real Estate Investment Trusts (REITs)**: For those who prefer not to manage properties directly, REITs offer a way to invest in real estate through a stock-like format. They pay dividends and are typically stable investments.

Diversifying Your Portfolio

Diversification is essential to managing risk and maximizing returns over time. Here's how to diversify effectively:

- **Across Asset Classes**: Include a mix of stocks, bonds, real estate, and possibly commodities or other alternative investments.

- **Geographically**: Invest in international markets in addition to your home country to reduce geographic risk and capitalize on growth in emerging markets.

- **By Sector and Industry**: Spread your investments across different sectors and industries to reduce the impact of sector-specific downturns.

Conclusion

Think of your investment portfolio as a garden that you cultivate over time. Just as a gardener selects a variety of plants to create a balanced ecosystem, so too should you diversify your investments to create a resilient financial landscape. This chapter has equipped you with the knowledge to plant the seeds of stocks, nurture the growth of bonds, and landscape with the sturdy structures of real estate investments.

As you tend your financial garden, remember that each investment choice you make should align not only with your financial goals but also with your personal comfort and risk tolerance. The world of investing is dynamic, and market conditions change like the seasons—sometimes predictably, sometimes not. Staying informed, adjusting your strategies as necessary, and maintaining a diversified portfolio will help you weather any storm.

Approach investing with curiosity and patience. Allow your investments the time they need to grow and mature, just as you would nurture a young sapling into a towering tree. Celebrate the milestones—when your dividends pay your monthly groceries or when your portfolio reaches that first significant sum. These are the fruits of your labor and strategy.

As you continue on your journey to FIRE, remember that investing is both an art and a science. It's a practice that can be refined over time with experience and education. So, keep learning, stay engaged with your investments, and enjoy the process of growing your wealth. Here's to a flourishing financial future that allows you the freedom and security to live your life on your terms.

CHAPTER 6

TAX OPTIMIZATION

Navigating the world of taxes might seem daunting, but understanding how to optimize your tax situation is akin to finding hidden treasure on your map to Financial Independence, Retire Early (FIRE). In this chapter, we'll delve into the various tax-advantaged accounts and strategies that not only comply with the law but also maximize your financial growth. Think of this as your guide to smart tax planning—ensuring every dollar you save on taxes is a dollar that works harder for you towards achieving early retirement.

Understanding Tax-Advantaged Accounts

Tax optimization plays a crucial role in accelerating your journey toward Financial Independence, Retire Early (FIRE). By utilizing tax-advantaged accounts, you can significantly reduce your taxable income and allow your investments to grow more efficiently.

• **401(k) and 403(b) Plans**: These employer-sponsored retirement accounts allow you to contribute pre-tax income, which reduces your taxable income. Earnings in these accounts grow tax-deferred until withdrawal in retirement.

• **Individual Retirement Accounts (IRAs)**: Both Traditional and Roth IRAs offer tax advantages. Contributions to Traditional IRAs may be tax-deductible, reducing your taxable income, while Roth IRAs provide tax-free growth and tax-free withdrawals in retirement.

- **Health Savings Accounts (HSAs)**: If you have a high-deductible health plan, an HSA allows you to make pre-tax contributions, which can be used tax-free for qualified medical expenses. This account also has the potential for investment growth.

Tax-Efficient Investment Strategies

Investing tax-efficiently involves selecting investment vehicles and strategies that minimize the tax burden over time.

- **Hold Investments Long-Term**: Long-term capital gains are taxed at a lower rate than short-term gains. By holding assets for over a year before selling, you can benefit from these lower rates.

- **Tax-Loss Harvesting**: This strategy involves selling investments at a loss to offset gains you've realized elsewhere in your portfolio. This can help reduce your overall capital gains tax liability.

- **Asset Location**: Utilize different account types (taxable vs. tax-advantaged) to hold investments in a manner that maximizes tax efficiency. For example, keep high-growth investments in Roth IRAs where gains can be withdrawn tax-free, and keep interest-generating bonds in tax-deferred accounts.

Leveraging Deductions and Credits

Understanding and taking full advantage of tax deductions and credits can further reduce your taxable income and enhance your savings.

- **Mortgage Interest Deduction**: If you own a home and itemize your deductions, the interest you pay on your mortgage can be deducted, which reduces your taxable income.

- **Charitable Contributions**: Donations to qualified charities are tax-deductible if you itemize your deductions. This not only supports good causes but also reduces your tax liability.

- **Education Credits**: The American Opportunity Tax Credit and Lifetime Learning Credit can help offset costs of education by reducing the amount of tax you owe on your return.

Planning for Tax Changes

Tax laws are subject to change, and staying informed about current and upcoming tax legislation is vital for effective tax planning.

- **Stay Informed**: Keep up with tax law changes by following reliable financial news sources, consulting with tax professionals, or using tax planning software.

- **Adjust Your Strategy**: As tax laws change, reevaluate and adjust your financial plans and investment strategies to continue optimizing for tax efficiency.

Conclusion

As we wrap up our exploration of tax optimization, remember that effective tax planning is much like gardening. Just as a gardener nourishes the soil and prunes the plants to yield a better harvest, so must you nurture your investments and trim any tax inefficiencies to cultivate a robust financial future. Embrace the complexity of tax laws as an opportunity to deepen your financial knowledge and empower yourself with the tools to grow your wealth more efficiently. By staying proactive and informed, you can turn the daunting maze of taxes into a strategic asset on your journey to FIRE. Each step you take in mastering tax optimization plants the seeds for a more fruitful financial independence, bringing your dreams of early retirement ever closer to reality.

CHAPTER 7

FRUGALITY AND MINIMALISM

Welcome to a chapter that's close to my heart—Frugality and Minimalism. As we embark on this journey toward Financial Independence, Retire Early (FIRE), it's crucial to reflect not just on how we save, but also on how we live. This chapter isn't about cutting corners or living a life of deprivation; rather, it's about embracing a lifestyle that enriches your existence while aligning with your financial goals.

Imagine waking up each day knowing that every aspect of your life—from the items in your home to the way you spend your money—is intentionally chosen to support your dreams and values. This chapter will guide you through the process of streamlining your life and finances in a way that brings joy, clarity, and freedom.

We'll explore practical strategies to distinguish between needs and wants, adopt sustainable spending habits, and cultivate a minimalist mindset that focuses on quality over quantity. By the end of this chapter, you'll see how living frugally can be a liberating and fulfilling path to achieving your dreams of early retirement and financial independence. Let's discover together how less can truly be more.

Embracing a Frugal Lifestyle

Frugality is a powerful tool on the path to Financial Independence, Retire Early (FIRE). It's about maximizing value with every dollar spent, ensuring that personal finance aligns with personal values. Here's a deeper look into cultivating a sustainable frugal lifestyle:

- **Understand Your Spending**: Begin with detailed tracking of all expenditures. Identify trends and areas where emotional or impulsive purchasing is prevalent. Tools like budgeting apps can automate this process, providing insights and alerts.

- **Set Spending Priorities**: Prioritize expenses that align with your long-term financial goals. Necessary expenses come first, but always evaluate if there's a more cost-effective option.

- **Embrace Cost-Saving Habits**: Develop habits that naturally lead to savings. Cook meals at home more often, use public transportation, and shop second-hand. These choices can drastically reduce monthly expenses without sacrificing quality of life.

Minimalist Living for Financial Independence

Minimalism complements frugality by promoting less consumption and focusing on what adds true value to your life. Here's how to integrate minimalism into your FIRE journey:

- **Purge Non-Essentials**: Go through your possessions and honestly assess what you use regularly. Sell or donate items that no longer serve a purpose in your life. This not only clears physical space but also mental space, reducing the urge to buy more.

- **One-In, One-Out Rule**: When a new item is purchased, an old one must go. This rule helps maintain a balanced number of possessions and discourages unnecessary accumulation.

- **Intentional Acquisitions**: Make each purchase a thoughtful decision. Avoid impulse buys by implementing a waiting period for all non-essential items to see if the urge to buy persists.

Distinguishing Needs from Wants

A critical aspect of both frugality and minimalism is clearly differentiating needs from wants:

- **Needs**: Basic requirements for a healthy and secure life—food, shelter, clothing, and healthcare. Evaluate choices within these categories for savings without compromising essential quality.

- **Wants**: Non-essential items that provide comfort, convenience, or luxury. Limit these expenses by questioning their true utility and joy they bring into your life.

- **Monthly Check-Ins**: Regularly review your expenditures on wants. See if these align with your happiness and FIRE goals. Adjust as necessary to prevent financial drift.

Living Frugally Without Feeling Deprived

The challenge in living frugally is to do so without feeling deprived:

- **Find Free or Low-Cost Entertainment**: Explore community events, local parks, or hobbies that require minimal investment. Libraries, for example, offer a wealth of free resources beyond books, including workshops, classes, and digital media.

- **Social Connections**: Strengthen relationships through activities that don't require substantial spending. Hosting potluck dinners, movie nights at home, or outdoor activities can enrich your social life without impacting your budget.

- **Reward Yourself**: Allocate a small part of your budget to treat yourself occasionally. This can be a modest outing, a small purchase, or an experience that feels like a splurge within your means.

Conclusion: The Richness of a Frugal and Minimalist Life

Adopting frugality and minimalism isn't just about saving money; it's about enriching your life by removing unnecessary distractions and focusing on what truly matters. As you simplify your lifestyle and spending, you'll find more space, time, and freedom to enjoy the things that are most important to you. This journey towards FIRE is not about deprivation but about finding a deeper satisfaction in living a life aligned with your core values. By embracing these principles, you set yourself on a path not just to financial independence, but to a genuinely fulfilling life.

CHAPTER 8

DEBT MANAGEMENT

Welcome to a chapter that many find crucial on their journey to Financial Independence, Retire Early (FIRE)—debt management. In this section, we'll explore how to transform what many see as a financial burden into a stepping stone towards your goals. Debt doesn't have to be a roadblock; with the right strategies and mindset, it can be managed and even leveraged to accelerate your progress towards financial freedom. Let's dive into practical, effective methods to control, reduce, and eliminate debt, turning a challenge into an opportunity for growth.

Strategies for Paying Off Debt

Effectively managing your debt is pivotal for freeing up financial resources that can be better used towards achieving FIRE. Here are specific strategies, complete with examples, to help you tackle debt efficiently:

- **Debt Avalanche Method**: Focus on paying off the debt with the highest interest rate first while maintaining minimum payments on others. For example, if you have credit card debt at 18% interest, a car loan at 5%, and a student loan at 3%, you would prioritize the credit card debt. This method reduces the amount you pay in interest over time, making it a cost-effective strategy.

- **Debt Snowball Method**: Start by clearing the smallest debt first, regardless of interest rates, while making minimum payments on larger debts. This could mean paying off a $500 medical bill before tackling a $2,000 credit card balance. The psychological win of paying off smaller debts can provide momentum and motivation to tackle larger debts.

- **Consolidation and Refinancing**: Combine multiple debts into one loan with a lower interest rate, or refinance a single debt to reduce the interest rate. For instance, if you have several high-interest credit card debts, consolidating them into a single personal loan with a lower interest rate can simplify your payments and reduce your interest burden. Similarly, refinancing a mortgage at a lower rate can decrease monthly payments and the total interest paid over the life of the loan.

Good Debt vs. Bad Debt

Understanding the difference between good and bad debt is essential for managing your finances wisely:

- **Good Debt**: This type of debt is taken on as an investment that is expected to increase your net worth or generate income over time. Examples include:

  o **Mortgage**: Borrowing to buy a home can be considered good debt, especially if the property value appreciates over time.

  o **Student Loans**: Investing in your education can lead to higher earning potential, classifying student loans as good debt.

  o **Business Loans**: These can help you expand a business, potentially increasing your income.

- **Bad Debt**: This involves borrowing for things that quickly lose value or do not contribute to increasing your wealth. Examples include:

  o **Credit Card Debt**: Often incurs high interest and is typically used for everyday purchases that depreciate quickly.

  o **Car Loans for Luxury Vehicles**: Cars depreciate in value rapidly, and luxury vehicles offer little in terms of investment returns.

- **Payday Loans**: These usually come with extremely high interest rates and are a risky financial burden.

Staying Debt-Free

Staying debt-free is a cornerstone in the journey toward Financial Independence, Retire Early (FIRE). When you are free from the burden of debt, you not only liberate your monthly budget from interest and payments, but you also gain the mental clarity and financial bandwidth to focus more effectively on wealth accumulation and investment. A debt-free status enhances your financial stability and reduces risk, allowing you to navigate economic downturns with greater resilience. This positioning is crucial because it enables more of your income to be directed towards savings and investments, compounding your growth potential. Additionally, living without debt aligns with the frugality and minimalism principles that underpin the FIRE movement, encouraging a lifestyle that prioritizes financial health and long-term security over immediate gratification. By maintaining a debt-free life, you set a strong foundation for building the wealth that will ultimately provide you the freedom to retire early and live on your own terms.

Maintaining a debt-free life involves adopting financial habits that prevent debt accumulation:

- **Emergency Fund**: Save up an emergency fund of three to six months' worth of expenses to cover unforeseen costs without going into debt.

- **Budgeting**: Keep a rigorous budget even after you're debt-free to ensure spending within your means.

- **Credit Use**: Utilize credit cards wisely. If you do use them, aim to pay off the full balance each month to avoid interest charges and maintain a good credit score.

Conclusion

As we conclude this chapter on debt management, remember that handling debt effectively is not just about eliminating what you owe, but also about making strategic decisions that align with your larger financial goals. By understanding and implementing these strategies, you're not just escaping debt; you're paving a clear path to financial independence and a secure, prosperous future. Let each decision and payment be a deliberate step towards realizing your dream of FIRE.

CHAPTER 9

HEALTHCARE PLANNING

Embarking on early retirement brings many exciting opportunities and a few intricate challenges—none more pivotal than securing healthcare. As you step into this new chapter of life ahead of traditional retirement age, figuring out how to cover medical needs without the cushion of employer benefits or Medicare becomes essential. In Chapter 9, we're diving deep into the world of healthcare planning for those who dare to retire early.

From understanding the maze of insurance options to managing healthcare costs and preparing for long-term care, this chapter is your roadmap. We'll explore how to maintain your health without compromising your financial goals, ensuring that medical bills are a manageable part of your budget rather than a threat to your freedom. Let's uncover the strategies that allow you to enjoy your hard-earned retirement with peace of mind, knowing you're well-prepared for whatever comes your way. Ready to tackle healthcare head-on? Let's get started!

Understanding Healthcare Options

As you pursue Financial Independence, Retire Early (FIRE), planning for healthcare is crucial. Unlike traditional retirees who may qualify for Medicare, early retirees need to navigate the complex landscape of healthcare options well before reaching the eligibility age for government benefits. Here's how to approach it:

- **Health Insurance Marketplaces**: Start by exploring state or federal health insurance exchanges. These platforms often provide a variety of plans, and you might qualify for subsidies based on your income, especially during the first years of retirement when income may drop.

- **Health Sharing Plans**: These are not insurance but can be a cost-effective alternative. Members share medical costs through a cooperative structure, often based on religious or ethical alignment.

- **Continuing Employer Coverage**: If you're leaving a job, look into COBRA for extending your employer-provided health insurance. Though expensive, it could be a viable short-term solution.

Managing Healthcare Costs

Controlling healthcare expenses is vital for maintaining your financial health in retirement. Here are strategies to manage these costs effectively:

- **High-Deductible Health Plans (HDHPs) with Health Savings Accounts (HSAs)**: HDHPs often have lower premiums. Pairing them with an HSA allows you to save pre-tax dollars, which can be used tax-free for qualified medical expenses, thereby extending your healthcare dollar.

- **Preventive Care**: Investing in preventive care can reduce long-term health costs. This includes regular check-ups, screenings, and vaccinations, which are often covered fully by health plans under current laws.

- **Lifestyle Choices**: Maintaining a healthy lifestyle through diet, exercise, and stress management can decrease healthcare costs by preventing diseases and health issues.

Long-Term Care Planning

Long-term care represents a significant potential financial risk. Here's how to prepare:

- **Long-Term Care Insurance**: Consider purchasing long-term care insurance, which can help cover the cost of care that regular health insurance, Medicare, or Medicaid might not cover, such as help with daily activities or nursing home care.

- **Hybrid Policies**: Some life insurance policies come with long-term care riders, which can be an effective way to handle two important financial planning issues with one product.

- **Savings and Investments**: Set aside a portion of your savings specifically for potential long-term care needs. This could be part of your overall investment strategy.

Conclusion

As we wrap up our journey through the essential world of healthcare planning in Chapter 9, remember that securing your health is as crucial as securing your financial future. The strategies we've discussed are not just about protecting your wallet—they're about ensuring that your retirement years are enjoyed to the fullest, unburdened by avoidable health costs and stress.

Taking the time now to understand your healthcare options, manage costs proactively, and plan for the unexpected ensures that you can focus on what truly matters in retirement—pursuing passions, exploring new hobbies, and spending time with loved ones. Health is the foundation upon which your retirement dreams are built, and with careful planning, it can be a cornerstone of your freedom, not a limitation.

Thank you for taking this important step in safeguarding your future. With a solid healthcare strategy in place, you're not just planning for early retirement; you're preparing for a vibrant, fulfilling, and worry-free adventure in your golden years. Let's move forward with confidence, knowing that your health, like your finances, is well cared for.

CHAPTER 10

RETIREMENT PLANNING

Welcome to Chapter 10, where we turn our dreams into plans. Retirement planning isn't just about making sure you have enough money to stop working; it's about creating a life in retirement that is as rich and fulfilling as the one you lived during your working years. This chapter is dedicated to guiding you through the intricate dance of calculating your needs, understanding safe withdrawal rates, and preparing for inflation so that you can craft a retirement that's not only financially secure but also truly enjoyable. Let's embark on this critical phase of your FIRE journey, where careful planning meets your biggest aspirations.

Calculating Your Retirement Number

The cornerstone of retirement planning is determining how much money you need to retire comfortably—your "retirement number." This figure is based on your expected annual spending, adjusted for inflation, and considering any other sources of income you might have in retirement, such as Social Security or a pension.

- **Annual Spending Needs**: Start by estimating your yearly expenses in retirement. Consider that some costs may decrease (like commuting expenses) while others may increase (like healthcare).

- **25x Rule**: A popular method within the FIRE community is the 25x rule, which suggests you should save 25 times your annual expenses to retire comfortably. For example, if you estimate your annual retirement expenses to be $40,000, according to the 25x rule, you would need to save $1,000,000 to sustainably fund your retirement. This is based on the assumption that you will withdraw 4% of your nest egg each year.

- **Adjust for Inflation**: Use historical inflation rates to project future expenses. Tools like inflation calculators can help you estimate the value of money in future terms.

Safe Withdrawal Rates

The Safe Withdrawal Rate (SWR) is the percentage of your portfolio that you can withdraw each year without running out of money. The traditional SWR is 4%, but this may need adjustment based on current economic conditions, your investment strategy, and how long you plan to be in retirement.

- **Longevity of Funds**: Consider a more conservative SWR if you plan an early retirement, as your funds need to last longer.

- **Market Conditions**: In volatile or bearish markets, you might need to adjust your withdrawal rate downwards to preserve capital.

Planning for Inflation

Inflation can erode the purchasing power of your savings, making it a critical factor in retirement planning. Here's how to safeguard against inflation:

- **TIPS**: Treasury Inflation-Protected Securities (TIPS) are government bonds that adjust for inflation and can provide a steady, risk-free return.

- **Diversification**: Investing in assets like real estate or stocks can provide returns that outpace inflation over the long term.

- **Flexible Spending Plan**: Have a plan to adjust your spending based on inflation rates and the performance of your investments.

Conclusion

As we close this chapter on retirement planning, remember that the goal is to transition smoothly into a retirement that brings you joy and peace of mind. Each calculation and plan you make now is a step toward securing that future. Armed with a robust strategy and a clear understanding of the challenges and opportunities ahead, you're well on your way to turning the golden years into some of the best years of your life. Let's continue to plan wisely, invest wisely, and look forward to the rewarding days ahead.

CHAPTER 11

PSYCHOLOGICAL ASPECTS OF FIRE

Embarking on the path to Financial Independence, Retire Early (FIRE) is often celebrated as a quest for financial savvy, but beneath the spreadsheets and savings plans, there's a deeply personal and emotional journey. This chapter delves into the less discussed, yet equally vital, psychological landscape of FIRE. It's not just about how much you save or invest; it's about how you navigate the feelings, relationships, and self-perceptions that evolve as you pursue this unconventional path.

Whether it's dealing with the raised eyebrows of skeptical relatives or the internal battle when passing up immediate pleasures for long-term gain, the journey to FIRE tests more than just your financial discipline. It challenges your resolve, reshapes your social interactions, and even redefines your personal identity. Here, we'll explore how to manage these dynamics effectively, ensuring your financial strides are matched with emotional resilience. Let's uncover the strategies that support not only a healthy bank account but also a fulfilled heart as you journey towards your FIRE goals.

Dealing with Social Pressures

The decision to pursue FIRE often deviates from societal norms about work, spending, and retirement, which can lead to misunderstandings or judgment from peers, family, or colleagues.

- **Communicating Your Choices**: Learn how to articulate your financial goals and decisions clearly to others to minimize misunderstandings or conflict. Share the benefits and your reasons for choosing this path, focusing on the positive aspects like freedom and security.

- **Building a Support System**: Surround yourself with like-minded individuals or online communities who share your goals and can offer support, advice, and encouragement. This network can be invaluable in maintaining your motivation and emotional well-being.

Maintaining Motivation

The path to FIRE can be long and requires sustained effort and discipline. Keeping your motivation high is crucial for long-term success.

- **Setting Short-Term Goals**: Break down your long-term financial goals into smaller, achievable milestones. Celebrating these achievements can provide ongoing motivation and a sense of progress.

- **Visualization**: Regularly visualize your life post-FIRE. Imagining your future can help reinforce why you're making current sacrifices and keep your goals vivid and compelling.

Mental Health and Financial Stress

Financial stress is a common experience for many, but when you're deeply involved in managing every penny for a goal like FIRE, it can become overwhelming.

- **Balance and Self-Care**: Ensure that you're not sacrificing your current well-being for future financial independence. Engage in activities that you enjoy and that relax you, and don't be afraid to occasionally treat yourself within budgeted limits.

- **Seek Professional Help**: If financial stress becomes too much, consider speaking with a financial advisor or a mental health professional. They can provide strategies to manage stress effectively and keep your mental health in check.

Creating a FIRE-Friendly Lifestyle

Living a lifestyle that supports your FIRE goals doesn't mean you have to live minimally or forego all pleasures—instead, it's about making strategic choices that align with your financial independence.

- **Mindful Spending**: Focus on spending money on experiences and items that truly add value to your life. This approach not only saves money but also enhances your quality of life.

- **Hobbies and Activities**: Engage in low-cost or free hobbies that enrich your life without detracting from your financial goals. Activities like hiking, reading, or volunteering can be fulfilling and inexpensive.

Conclusion

The journey to FIRE is as much a psychological journey as a financial one. By understanding the emotional aspects and preparing for them, you can ensure that your path to financial independence is not only successful but also enjoyable. Remember, the goal of FIRE is not just to escape from something (like a job you dislike) but to move towards something—a life filled with freedom, purpose, and contentment. Keep your mental and emotional health in balance with your financial goals, and you'll be able to enjoy every step of the journey to reaching your FIRE aspirations.

CHAPTER 12

CREATING A FIRE-FRIENDLY LIFESTYLE

As we journey towards Financial Independence, Retire Early (FIRE), it becomes essential to cultivate a lifestyle that not only supports this ambitious goal but enriches our daily lives. Achieving FIRE isn't solely about reaching financial milestones; it's about creating a sustainable, enjoyable way of living that continues to inspire and motivate us. In this chapter, we'll explore how to harmoniously blend life's pleasures with prudent financial habits, fostering a lifestyle that feels both rewarding and responsible.

Building a Supportive Community

The path to FIRE can sometimes feel lonely or misunderstood by those not sharing the same journey. Building a community of like-minded individuals can provide not only emotional support but also practical advice and motivation.

- **Engage with Online Communities**: Join forums, social media groups, and blogs where people share their FIRE experiences and strategies. These platforms can be invaluable for encouragement, advice, and learning.

- **Local Meetups and Clubs**: Look for or start local meetups with others interested in personal finance and investing. Regular meetings can help keep you accountable and inspired.

- **Family Involvement**: Involve your family in your FIRE plans. Discussing goals and budgets helps ensure everyone understands and supports the lifestyle adjustments that may be necessary.

Staying Active and Engaged

Maintaining an active and fulfilling life is crucial for long-term sustainability on the FIRE path. It's important to find joy in activities beyond the financial grind.

- **Pursue Hobbies That Pay Off**: Engage in hobbies that are not only enjoyable but can also be monetarily beneficial. Activities like gardening, blogging about your FIRE journey, or woodworking can potentially generate extra income.

- **Volunteer Your Time**: Volunteering can offer a sense of purpose and fulfillment that money can't buy. Find causes you care about and contribute your time or skills.

- **Lifelong Learning**: Continue to educate yourself, not just about finance but also other areas of interest. Online courses, workshops, and books can keep you intellectually stimulated and personally satisfied.

Adjusting Lifestyle Costs

Living a FIRE-friendly lifestyle often means finding smart ways to reduce expenses without compromising on the quality of life.

- **Frugal Living Tips**: Adopt frugal habits that don't feel like sacrifices. This could mean mastering the art of cooking delicious, cost-effective meals at home, learning basic home maintenance, or embracing secondhand shopping.

- **Minimalist Living**: Embrace minimalism in a way that makes sense for your life. This isn't about deprivation but about focusing on what adds real value to your life.

- **Energy Efficiency**: Implement energy-saving measures at home, such as LED lighting, energy-efficient appliances, and smart thermostats, which can significantly reduce utility bills.

Conclusion

Creating a FIRE-friendly lifestyle is about more than just saving money and investing wisely; it's about building a life that you don't need a vacation from. It's about crafting a day-to-day existence that aligns with your values and your long-term financial goals, while also being rich in experiences and personal growth. By embracing community support, staying actively engaged in fulfilling activities, and managing lifestyle costs, you set the stage for a sustainable journey towards financial independence that is as enjoyable as the destination itself. Let this chapter be your guide in molding a lifestyle that not only leads to early retirement but also enhances every moment along the way.

CHAPTER 13

TOOLS AND RESOURCES FOR ACHIEVING FIRE

As you forge ahead on your journey to Financial Independence, Retire Early (FIRE), having the right tools and resources at your disposal can make all the difference. This chapter is your toolkit, packed with essential resources that can streamline your path, enhance your financial literacy, and optimize your investment strategies. Whether you're just starting out or are well into your FIRE journey, these tools will help keep you informed, organized, and motivated.

Financial Independence Calculators

Understanding the numbers behind your financial decisions is vital. Here are some top calculators that can help you plan and track your progress:

- **FIRE Simulators**: Tools like FIRECalc or cFIREsim allow you to test your retirement strategy against historical data to see how well your savings would have held up during past economic conditions.

- **Savings Rate Calculators**: Quickly determine how changes in your savings rate could affect the time it takes to reach financial independence.

- **Compound Interest Calculators**: Visualize how your investments could grow over time with tools like the compound interest calculators available on websites like Investor.gov or MoneyChimp.

Sample FIRE Tracker Template

As you navigate the intricate path towards Financial Independence, Retire Early (FIRE), having robust tools to monitor your progress is indispensable. This is where our sample FIRE Tracker Template comes into play—an essential resource designed to keep your financial goals in sharp focus and your strategies on track.

In this template, we've distilled complex financial concepts into an easy-to-use spreadsheet format. Whether you're tracking monthly expenses, calculating your savings rate, overseeing your investment portfolio, marking milestones, or evaluating your net worth, this template serves as your personal finance dashboard. It's not just about logging numbers; it's about understanding your financial journey at a glance and making informed decisions based on that insight.

Let's dive into this template, where each tab and column has been carefully crafted to help you effectively manage your finances. By integrating this tool into your daily financial practices, you'll enhance your ability to not only reach but also sustain your FIRE objectives. Ready to transform your financial data into a powerful ally on your journey to freedom? Let's get started.

Sheet 1: Monthly Budget Tracker

Date	Category	Planned Amount	Actual Amount	Difference
2024-07-01	Housing	$1,000	$1,000	$0
2024-07-01	Groceries	$300	$285	$15
2024-07-01	Transportation	$150	$150	$0
2024-07-01	Entertainment	$100	$120	-$20
...	...	...	...	...

Sheet 2: Savings Rate Calculator

Month	Total Income	Total Savings	Savings Rate (%)
July 2024	$5,000	$2,000	40%
August 2024	$5,000	$2,100	42%

Sheet 3: Investment Portfolio Summary

Investment Type	Amount Invested	Current Value	Returns
Stocks	$10,000	$10,500	5%
Bonds	$5,000	$5,200	4%
Real Estate	$20,000	$21,000	5%
...	...	...	...

Sheet 4: FIRE Milestone Tracker

Milestone	Target Date	Status	Notes
$100K Net Worth	Dec 2025	On Track	Next review in Dec 2024
Debt-Free	Jun 2024	Achieved	Paid off final student loan
$500K Investment	Jan 2030	On Track	Consider increasing savings
...	...	...	...

Sheet 5: Net Worth Calculator

Date	Total Assets	Total Liabilities	Net Worth
July 2024	$50,000	$20,000	$30,000
August 2024	$51,000	$19,500	$31,500

Instructions for Use

- **Monthly Budget Tracker**: Update this sheet regularly with your expenses to monitor and manage your spending habits.

- **Savings Rate Calculator**: Update monthly after all income and savings figures are known.

- **Investment Portfolio Summary**: Review and update quarterly to reflect current values and adjust as needed based on performance and financial goals.

- **FIRE Milestone Tracker**: Check and update during your regular financial reviews, whether monthly, quarterly, or annually, to track progress towards specific financial milestones.

- **Net Worth Calculator**: Update monthly to keep a clear view of your financial health and progress.

Visualization

Consider using conditional formatting or charts within the spreadsheet to visually map the growth of investments, trends in savings rates, and net worth over time. This can provide motivational insights into how your financial strategies are performing.

This template provides a structured approach to tracking your finances, helping ensure that you are on the right path to achieving your FIRE goals.

Recommended Books and Blogs

Continuing education is crucial in maintaining momentum and staying inspired. Here are some must-read books and blogs that offer valuable insights and strategies:

- **Books**:

  o *"Your Money or Your Life"* by Vicki Robin and Joe Dominguez — a foundational read for understanding the philosophy behind financial independence.

  o *"The Simple Path to Wealth"* by JL Collins — offers straightforward advice on investing and financial planning.

  o *"Early Retirement Extreme"* by Jacob Lund Fisker — explores how radical savings can accelerate your journey to FIRE.

- **Blogs**:

  o Mr. Money Mustache — features a wealth of articles on practical frugality and investing for early retirement.

  o Mad Fientist — provides detailed financial strategies and tools for reaching financial independence sooner.

  o Financial Samurai — offers in-depth analysis of investment strategies and financial trends.

Useful Apps and Software

Leverage technology to manage your finances more effectively with these helpful apps and software:

- **Budgeting and Tracking**:

  o **Mint**: Helps track your spending and budget, and offers custom recommendations for saving money.

  o **You Need A Budget (YNAB)**: Emphasizes planning your spending and adjusting as you go, which is perfect for the dynamic nature of managing finances on a FIRE path.

- **Investment Management**:

  o **Personal Capital**: A comprehensive tool that not only tracks spending but also provides detailed insights into your investment portfolio performance.

  o **Vanguard** or **Fidelity Apps**: Manage your investments directly and make use of their extensive resources and research tools.

Forums and Online Communities

Engaging with others on the same path can provide support, ideas, and motivation. Here are some forums where you can connect with fellow FIRE enthusiasts:

- **Reddit**: Subreddits like r/financialindependence and r/FIRE offer a platform to discuss strategies, successes, challenges, and more.

- **Early Retirement Forums**: A long-standing community where seasoned and novice FIRE pursuers share insights and encouragement.

Conclusion

As we conclude this chapter, remember that the journey to FIRE is unique for each individual but having access to a robust set of tools and resources can provide a common foundation for success. Whether through learning from others' experiences, tracking your progress with sophisticated tools, or finding inspiration in a community, these resources are your allies. Equip yourself with knowledge, stay connected with like-minded individuals, and use these tools to navigate your path to financial independence and early retirement with confidence and clarity.

CHAPTER 14

CONCLUSION

As we prepare to close this chapter on your journey towards Financial Independence, Retire Early (FIRE), let's take a moment to reflect on the road we've traveled together. From the nuts and bolts of financial planning to the inspiring tales of those who've successfully navigated this path, each page has been a step toward not just understanding but envisioning your life of freedom. This concluding chapter is more than just a recap; it's a compass for staying true to your course, continuing to learn and adapt, and ultimately living a life brimming with fulfillment and independence. So, let's gather these valuable insights, celebrate your progress, and look forward to the exciting possibilities that your future holds.

Staying the Course

As we conclude our exploration of the diverse and inspiring journeys to Financial Independence, Retire Early (FIRE), it's essential to underscore the importance of persistence. Staying the course, despite the inevitable challenges and setbacks, is a cornerstone of every successful FIRE journey. The path is rarely linear, and it often requires enduring periods of financial uncertainty, market volatility, or personal doubt. However, the resolve to keep pushing forward—guided by a well-defined financial plan and clear personal goals—is what ultimately separates those who reach their FIRE aspirations from those who falter. Remember, consistency in saving, investing wisely, and living within your means can compound into substantial long-term success.

Continual Learning and Adaptation

The landscape of personal finance and investment is continually evolving, and so too should your strategies and knowledge. The stories we've shared highlight that continual learning and the willingness to adapt are vital traits of successful FIRE participants. Whether it's adapting to new tax laws, shifting investment strategies in response to economic changes, or refining budgets to better meet your changing life circumstances, flexibility is key. Engage with new learning opportunities, whether through books, blogs, webinars, or conversations with fellow FIRE enthusiasts. This ongoing education will not only help you adjust your strategies but will also keep you motivated and engaged with your financial goals.

Living a Fulfilled and Independent Life

Ultimately, the goal of FIRE is not merely to escape the traditional workforce but to gain the freedom to live a fulfilled and independent life on your own terms. This means having the financial security to make choices that align with your values, passions, and life goals. Whether that involves traveling the world, pursuing hobbies, volunteering, or spending more time with family, FIRE opens a realm of possibilities.

The fulfillment that comes from living independently should also include a balance of mental and physical well-being. As you work toward your financial goals, remember to maintain a healthy lifestyle, nurture relationships, and keep a supportive community around you. These elements are crucial for enjoying the fruits of your labor when you finally achieve FIRE.

Wrapping Up

The journey to FIRE is both challenging and deeply rewarding. As you close this chapter and continue on your path, carry with you the lessons of persistence, adaptability, and the pursuit of fulfillment. Stay the course with diligence, embrace change with flexibility, and look forward to the freedom and satisfaction that come with achieving financial independence. Here's to your success on this exciting journey to a life of financial freedom and personal enrichment.

SPECIAL THANKS

A heartfelt thank you to all who have made this book possible—from family and friends who provided unwavering support, to the community of FIRE enthusiasts who shared their inspiring stories. This journey would not have been as rich or fulfilling without your contributions and encouragement.

Note from Dr. Denise Greaves

I am deeply grateful for the opportunity to share this journey with you. My hope is that this book not only guides you to financial independence but also inspires you to reimagine what your life can be. Remember, the path to FIRE is not a race, but a journey to be savored. Each step you take is a step towards a life of freedom and choice.

Connect with Me:

- **Email**: drdenisewrites@gmail.com

FIRE Expense Tracker: Manual Receipt Collection for Financial Independence

If you're serious about managing your finances as you journey towards financial independence, you may also want to consider purchasing the *FIRE Expense Tracker: Manual Receipt Collection for Financial Independence*. This companion notebook is specifically designed to help you meticulously track your spending by organizing and storing your receipts. It's an invaluable tool for anyone committed to a detailed and disciplined approach to budgeting, making it easier to monitor expenditures, analyze financial habits, and stay on track with your FIRE goals.

Thank you for choosing *Pathways to FIRE*. Here's to your success on the road to financial independence and early retirement!

www.ingramcontent.com/pod-product-compliance
Lightning Source LLC
Chambersburg PA
CBHW070209100426
42743CB00013B/3108